PROJECT

CODE

CREATE COMPUTER GAMES
WITH SCRATCH

Illustrated by
Glen McBeth

Kevin Wood

W
FRANKLIN WATTS
LONDON • SYDNEY

Franklin Watts
First published in Great Britain in 2017 by
The Watts Publishing Group

Copyright © The Watts Publishing
Group 2017

Credits
Editor: Julia Adams/Julia Bird
Series Designer: Alix Wood
Cover Designer: Peter Scoulding
Illustrations: Glen McBeth

Every attempt has been made to clear copyright.
Should there be any inadvertent omission please
apply to the publisher for rectification.

Speech bubble designed by Freepik

ISBN: 978 1 4451 5596 8

Printed in China

Franklin Watts
An imprint of
Hachette Children's Group
Part of The Watts Publishing Group
Carmelite House
50 Victoria Embankment
London EC4Y 0DZ

An Hachette UK Company
www.hachette.co.uk

www.franklinwatts.co.uk

MIX
Paper from
responsible sources
FSC
www.fsc.org
FSC® C104740

Using Scratch

Scratch is a programming language designed by MIT (Massachusetts Institute of Technology) that
lets you create your own interactive stories, animations, games, music and art. Rather than using
a complex computer language, it uses easy-to-understand coding blocks. To get the most out of
this book, you will need to be able to use a computer and you will need to load Scratch onto your
computer. Always check with an adult if it is OK to download files from the Internet to your computer.
Go to: **https://scratch.mit.edu**

First, do Scratch's 'Getting Started with Scratch' tutorial, found by going to 'Create' on the home page,
and then look in the 'Tips' menu. You can also work on Scratch offline. Scroll to the bottom
of the homepage and click on Offline Editor in the Support menu. Follow the instructions
to install it on your computer.

CONTENTS

To load the projects that you will use in this book, go to:

www.alixwoodbooks.co.uk/projectcode/downloads.php

and select 'Games'. Save the folder somewhere on your computer where you will be able to find it again. You will need to open files in this folder as you go through the project.

Words in **bold** are in the glossary on page 30.

ALL ABOUT COMPUTER GAMES

Do you like computer games? Perhaps you like puzzles, action games or adventure games. Have you ever wondered how people write computer games? You can create games yourself using a program called Scratch.

Planning your computer game

Before you write a computer game you need to decide a few things. What kind of game do you want to write? What will the aim of the game be? Will your game have characters? What will the characters do?

Once you have a plan, Scratch helps you create games easily using pieces of **code**, called coding blocks. The blocks can be arranged to create different kinds of programs, such as games.

Starting from Scratch

To get some inspiration, have a look at some of the games that people have shared on the Scratch website. You can click on the 'see inside' button to look at the code.

https://scratch.mit.edu/starter_projects/#Games

Try it!

How about making a simple dressing-up game to play with your friends? Open our game called dressing.sb2 to see one we have created. Or you can try making one yourself:

1 In Scratch, you can choose backgrounds known as backdrops for your game. Click on 'New backdrop'. You can choose a backdrop from the library, draw your own, or upload one from your computer or camera.

2 Now you need someone to dress. Choose a **sprite** from the library. Sprites are characters in Scratch that you can write code for. Go to 'New sprite', and choose 'Dress-Up' from the menu on the left under 'Theme'. You'll see a sprite called Dani and some clothes that will fit her. Select the clothes you want and click 'OK'.

3 To play the game, simply drag and drop the clothes onto Dani!

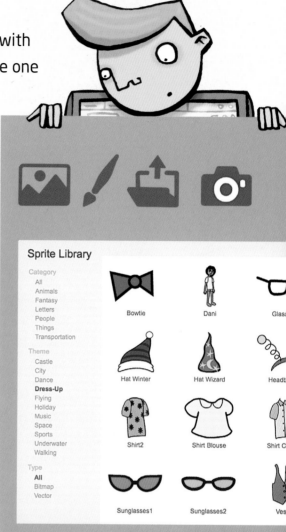

Sprite Library

Category
All
Animals
Fantasy
Letters
People
Things
Transportation

Theme
Castle
City
Dance
Dress-Up
Flying
Holiday
Music
Space
Sports
Underwater
Walking

Type
All
Bitmap
Vector

Bowtie   Dani   Glass

Hat Winter   Hat Wizard   Headb

Shirt2   Shirt Blouse   Shirt C

Sunglasses1   Sunglasses2   Ves

PROJECT PAGE:
KEEPING SCORE

>>> The dressing-up game was fun, but it wasn't that exciting. Games work well when they have challenges, for example when you need to beat somebody else, collect points or do something in a short space of time. Let's try to make a game with challenges, so that it's more **competitive**. >>>

How am I doing?

When you play a competitive game it is useful to know your score, so you can see how well you are doing. Try creating this simple reactions game. Open basketball.sb2. The player has to try to catch the basketball by clicking on it each time it appears on the screen. The player's score is displayed in the top left-hand corner of the screen. Click on the green flag to start the game.

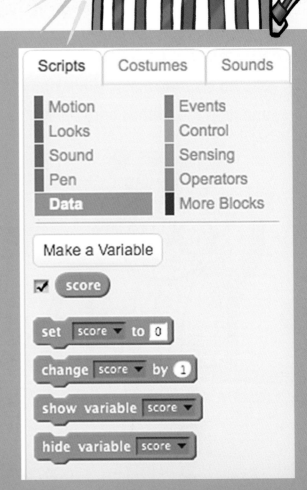

1 To create the scoreboard for this game, click on your chosen sprite, in this case, the basketball. Go to '**Data**' and click on 'Make a **Variable**'. Type 'score' and your score choices will appear, like this:

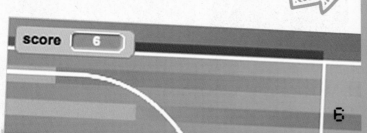

2 Now you can use the different scoring elements in your game. For this basketball game we change the score by 1 each time the sprite is clicked. When a new game starts, we set the score back to 0.

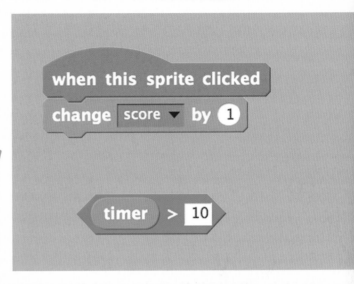

3 This game uses a timer. If we didn't put the timer in our code, the game would play for ever! You can change how long the game goes on for by changing the value in the timer. At the moment, the game lasts for 10 seconds.

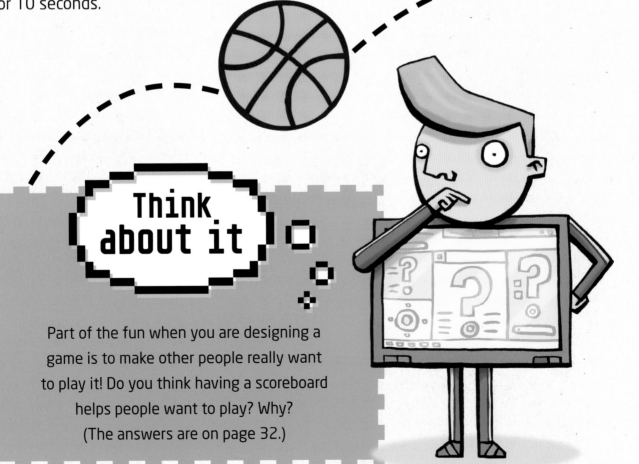

Think about it

Part of the fun when you are designing a game is to make other people really want to play it! Do you think having a scoreboard helps people want to play? Why?

(The answers are on page 32.)

USING LOOPS

In Scratch, you can create a loop to:
- repeat the code forever
- repeat the code a number of times
- repeat the code until something else happens.

To do this in Scratch, you use the FOREVER, REPEAT or REPEAT UNTIL blocks.

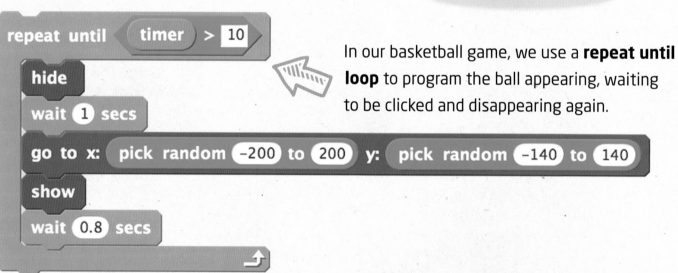

In our basketball game, we use a **repeat until loop** to program the ball appearing, waiting to be clicked and disappearing again.

Without the repeat until loop, we would have to tell the basketball sprite to hide, wait, appear in a **random** place, hide, wait and appear, over and over again. Using the repeat loop above tells the computer to repeat the same action until the time runs out, so we don't have to write the same piece of code more than once.

To make the game last longer, adjust the value next to the timer in the 'Repeat until' block.

AHA!

Try it

See if you can adjust the code in this game to make the game easier or harder. Try changing the second 'wait' value inside the forever loop. If the number is larger, say 1, the ball will be on screen for a little longer. If you make the number smaller, say 0.5, the ball will be on the screen for a shorter time, making the game harder. You can also adjust the first wait value to make the ball appear quicker each time.

Adding sounds

You can add sounds to your game. Click on the 'Sound' scripts and you'll see you can play sounds and musical instruments, and change their volume and tempo (speed). To select a sound, you need to go to the Scratch Sound Library.

There are all kinds of fun sounds that would be great for different games. Click on them to hear what they sound like, and choose some for your game.

ARCADE GAMES

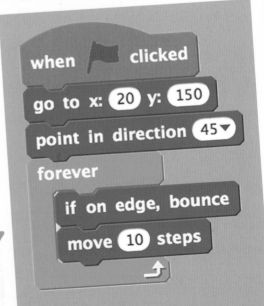

>>> Arcade games are the types of computer games played in amusement arcades. They are often shooting games, or pinball-type games.

One of the earliest and most popular arcade games was called Pong. It was a table tennis game where the aim was to keep a ball in play. You can make a game like Pong using Scratch.

Paddleball

1 Open paddleball.sb2. In this game you operate a paddle with your mouse. You use the paddle to keep the ball from landing on the red line. If the ball touches the line the game is over. Start the game by clicking on the green flag.

How did you do? Was the game too easy or too hard? Let's look at all the things we can change in the game to make it more or less difficult.

2 Click on the ball sprite to look at its code. The first piece of code tells the ball what position on the screen to start from. (You can read more about x and y positions on page 17). Inside our forever loop, the 'If on edge, bounce' block tells our ball not to go off the edge of the screen.

```
when [flag] clicked
go to x: 20 y: 150
point in direction 45▼
forever
    if on edge, bounce
    move 10 steps
```

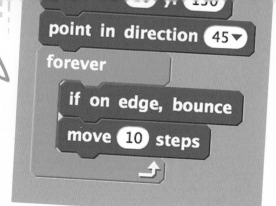

```
point in direction 45 ▾
forever
    if on edge, bounce
    move 10 steps
```

3 The 'Move' block adjusts the speed at which the ball will travel. At the moment the value is set to 10. If you want the ball to move faster, type a higher value, such as 15, in the box. If you want it to go slower, lower the value. Try the game again and see how you do.

```
when 🏳 clicked
forever
    if   touching color ■ ?   then
        stop all ▾
```

You could change what happens when the ball hits the red line, too. At the moment the 'Stop all' block just makes the game stop. Maybe you could add a groan sound using a 'play sound' block, too.

AHA!

Try it

What if you want to use a different ball or add a second ball to your game? Choose a new ball sprite. Copy the code from your original ball by right-clicking on each code block and selecting 'duplicate'. Drag the duplicate code onto the new sprite. The blocks may appear on top of each other so you might need to tidy them up.

Delete the original ball and just use your new one, or try using two balls. It's much harder! We added the Earth to our space-themed Paddleball. Open paddleball2.sb2 to try out this version.

STRATEGY GAMES

A strategy game invites the player to make choices which affect what happens next. Chess is a strategy game. Every piece that you move in chess makes a big difference to what happens in the game. These games are won through tactics. A lot of computer war games are strategy games.

Dragons

For this book, we have created a strategy game called Dragons. Our hero is a little frog that we need to save from an increasing number of nasty dragons. If you like, you can play the finished game first, so that you can see what we are going to create. Open dragons.sb2 in Scratch and click on the green flag. The game looks better if you go to full screen mode.

How to play the game

You can move the frog one space in any direction using the arrow keys on your keyboard. Be careful not to make the frog fall into a hole, though. After the frog has moved, all of the dragons will take one step towards it. Watch out! They will eat the frog if they catch it. When you have beaten all the dragons you go up to a new level. See how long you can keep the frog alive!

Dragon slaying

You can get rid of the dragons by making them fall into a hole, or crash into each other. When they crash into each other, they create a new hole.

AHA!

Tips:
- Hide behind a hole to lure the dragons towards it!
- Try moving using the keyboard. Use keys W, A, D and X. To go up, press W; to move down, press X; to go left, press A; and to go right, press D.
- You can move diagonally using Q, E, Z or C. You can remain still by pressing the S key.

If you look at the code, you will see that there is a lot of it! It may look very complicated at the moment, but don't worry. We will go through it bit by bit, building it up as we go.

MAKING DECISIONS

>>> Now we are going to begin to create our own Dragons game. Let's start by looking at how our main character, the frog, will move around the screen. Open dragons1.sb2 in Scratch and click the green flag. >>>

You can see that we have divided the screen into a **grid** of 18 rows and 24 columns. Each square is called a cell and is 20 **pixels** high and 20 pixels wide. At the start, the frog sits in a cell in the middle of the grid.

Waiting for instructions ...

This part of our code needs to make three decisions. It is waiting for the green flag to be clicked, waiting for a key to be pressed and deciding which key has been pressed. The code is only activated if one of the arrow keys has been pressed. If it has, the frog moves to the left, right, up or down 20 spaces (or pixels), which is the same as one cell.

```
when any ▼ key pressed
if      key  right arrow ▼  pressed?  then
    change x by 20
if      key  left arrow ▼  pressed?  then
    change x by -20
if      key  up arrow ▼  pressed?  then
```

How do we make decisions in code?

We can use an IF statement to make decisions. The IF statement is one of the most used statements in coding. It allows the code to make a decision by asking IF something has happened. For example, IF an arrow key is pressed, THEN the code moves the frog in the direction of the arrow key. IF no arrow key is pressed, nothing will happen.

Think about it

Being able to make decisions makes code seem more human. If you programmed a robot to walk forwards, it would walk forwards even if there was a cliff edge in front of it. A person would make the decision to stop if they saw the drop! If you programmed the robot to 'walk forwards IF no cliff edge' they would make the same decision as the person.

Coding unplugged

You make IF decisions every day. If your arm is itchy, you'll scratch it. For a computer to make the decision to scratch, it needs to be told its arm is itchy, and told to scratch as a result. Try this IF game and turn your decisions into code. Write down six things you must do, such as 'eat a biscuit' or 'do my homework' and number them 1–6. Now roll a die. To run your code you must do the thing you wrote next to that number.

OPERATORS

Now that you can move the frog around the screen, you may notice that it is possible to move him off the screen entirely. We don't really want this, so let's add some code to stop it from happening. Open dragons2.sb2 in Scratch.

You will see that we have added an extra IF statement to each 'Key pressed' one. Before the frog moves, the code needs to check whether there is a cell for the frog to move to. For this second IF statement, we need to use an **operator**.

Tip: Adding a green operator block can be fiddly. Hover over the space until it glows white, then drop it in place.

Different types of operator

Computer operators control how the computer uses data. Data are numbers or other information that we type into the computer or select on-screen. When we type a number into our computer, the operator tells the computer what to do with it.

There are a few different types of operator:

- Maths operators let us perform simple maths such as 'add +', 'subtract -', 'multiply x' and 'divide ÷'.

- Comparison operators compare values, and are operators such as 'less than' (shown as <), 'greater than' (shown as >) or 'equal to' (shown as =).

- Logic operators are explained in the next chapter: they are operators such as AND, OR and NOT.

Using comparison operators

In our project we use the comparison operators 'greater than' and 'less than'. If the player asks to move the frog right, the operator tells the computer to only move the frog if its current position ('X') is less than 220 (the edge of the screen). The operator makes sure there is space for the frog to move right. If there is, the frog can be moved. If there isn't, the frog stays where it is. Try moving the frog off the screen using the arrow keys. You should no longer be able to do so.

Think about it

Asking if something is 'less than' or 'greater than' is really useful in coding. Imagine a game in which the player has to get a certain score before they can go to the next level. You might use a 'greater than' operator – the player can only move to the next level when their score is greater than the score needed.

AHA!

x2; y3

What are X and Y?

All graphs and grids have an x-axis and a y-axis. They help you describe where a point is on a grid. The **horizontal axis is** the x-axis. The **vertical axis is** the y-axis. Each time the frog moves, we adjust the X and Y values of the frog to pinpoint where he is.

Try it!

Now you can move the frog around the screen, you could make a maze game. Click on the 'New backdrop' paintbrush. Create a maze using the rectangle tool. Perhaps you could add a timer, and make a clapping sound when you reach the exit. Open maze. sb2 and try to steer the frog to the exit, marked by a green cell.

PROJECT PAGE:
THIS OR THAT?

>>> You may have noticed in the full Dragons game that you could use many different keys to move the frog. People have different types of keyboard and some of them don't have arrow keys that can be used for games. In dragons2.sb2 we could only use the arrow keys. >>>

Open dragons3.sb2 in Scratch. Now you can use many different keys to move up, down, left and right. We can use a block of letter keys from the left side of the keyboard, or the arrow keys.

To make sure the code allows all the different keys, we need to use the logic operator 'OR'. This operator allows us to list all the different keys we would like to be able to use to make the frog move in a particular direction.

```
when  any ▼  key  pressed

if      key  right arrow ▼  pressed?    or    key  d ▼  pressed?    then
    if        x position  < 220  then
        change x by 20



if      key  left arrow ▼  pressed?    or    key  a ▼  pressed?    then
    if        x position  > -240  then
```

Logic operators

Logic operators use Boolean logic. Boolean logic is named after a man called George Boole. Boole invented a really simple system of logic, where every question can be answered with either 'true' or 'false'. The answer to 'Am I itchy?' is either 'yes' (true) or 'no' (false). Logic operators can also use Boolean logic to answer more complex questions by using AND and OR. For example, if you wanted to know 'Am I itchy OR hot?', the operator would check which of the conditions (itchy or hot) is true.

OR logic

OR logic tests to see if one of the conditions is true. For example: 'IF I press the right arrow OR I press the 'D' key THEN move the frog to the right.' If the answer to either question is true then the frog is moved one cell to the right.

AND logic

AND logic tests to see if the answers to both questions are true. For example: 'If I press the right arrow key AND there is space to the right of the frog, THEN move the frog to the right.' If the answer to either question is 'no', then the frog won't move.

Think about it

Does this statement use OR logic or AND logic? 'If I press the 7 key and there is space to move up and left, then move up and left.'
(The answers are on page 32.)

COORDINATES AND VARIABLES

It is important in the game to know which cell the frog is in, as well as which cells have holes or dragons. To keep track of the cells, we need to use a number of variables.

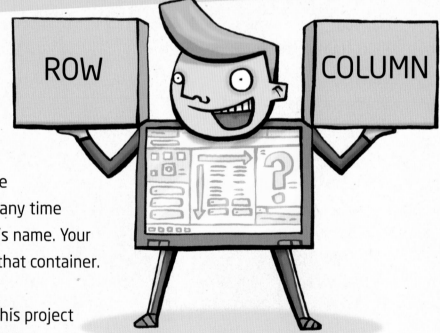

Storage containers

Variables are values that can be changed. A variable is a little like a container for data. You name your variable and store data in it. You can use that data any time you want by typing the variable's name. Your code will then fetch the data in that container.

Open dragons4.sb2 in Scratch. This project operates just like the last one, but the code is quite different. We have now used variables. In our 'Row' variable block we have entered the value 9. In our 'Column' (col) variable box we have entered the value 12. These values place the frog in the centre cell of the grid. 'Row', 'Col' and 'Cell' are variables, because you can change them by altering the values in the white boxes.

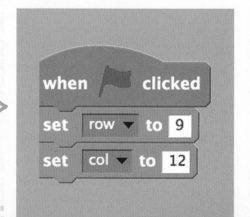

```
set  Cell ▼  to  ( row * 24 + col )
```

AHA!

This piece of code uses variables to give each cell a number. It works like this. There are 24 columns. Each cell on the bottom row (0) is given its number by multiplying the row number (0) by 24 and then adding its column number.

Let's work out the cell number of the green cross on our grid: 0 (row number) x 24 = 0; 0 + 0 (column number) = 0, so the cell number is '0'. For the blue cross, the sum is: 1 (row number) x 24 = 24; 24 + 1 (column number) = 25; the cell next to it would be 24 + 2 = 26 and so on, all the way to the top right cell, which is number 431.

See if you can work out the cell number for some other grid positions. Check the table below to see if you were right.

Try it!

Try getting the frog to start from different positions on the grid. Type a number between 0 and 23 in the column variable and 0-17 in the row variable. Can you predict which square your frog will start in? The numbers go from 0-17 and 0-23, but there are 18 rows and 24 columns. Why?

(The answers are on page 32.)

	0	1	2	3	4	5	6	7	8	9	10	11	12	13	14	15	16	17	18	19	20	21	22	23
17	408	409	410	411	412	413	414	415	416	417	418	419	420	421	422	423	424	425	426	427	428	429	430	431
16	384	385	386	387	388	389	390	391	392	393	394	395	396	397	398	399	400	401	402	403	404	405	406	407
15	360	361	362	363	364	365	366	367	368	369	370	371	372	373	374	375	376	377	378	379	380	381	382	383
14	336	337	338	339	340	341	342	343	344	345	346	347	348	349	350	351	352	353	354	355	356	357	358	359
13	312	313	314	315	316	317	318	319	320	321	322	323	324	325	326	327	328	329	330	331	332	333	334	335
12	288	289	290	291	292	293	294	295	296	297	298	299	300	301	302	303	304	305	306	307	308	309	310	311
11	264	265	266	267	268	269	270	271	272	273	274	275	276	277	278	279	280	281	282	283	284	285	286	287
10	240	241	242	243	244	245	246	247	248	249	250	251	252	253	254	255	256	257	258	259	260	261	262	263
9	216	217	218	219	220	221	222	223	224	225	226	227	228	229	230	231	232	233	234	235	236	237	238	239
8	92	193	194	195	196	197	198	199	200	201	202	203	204	205	206	207	208	209	210	211	212	213	214	215
7	68	169	170	171	172	173	174	175	176	177	178	179	180	181	182	183	184	185	186	187	188	189	190	191
6	144	145	146	147	148	149	150	151	152	153	154	155	156	157	158	159	160	161	162	163	164	165	166	167
5	120	121	122	123	124	125	126	127	128	129	130	131	132	133	134	135	136	137	138	139	140	141	142	143
4	96	97	98	99	100	101	102	103	104	105	106	107	108	109	110	111	112	113	114	115	116	117	118	119
3	72	73	74	75	76	77	78	79	80	81	82	83	84	85	86	87	88	89	90	91	92	93	94	95
2	48	49	50	51	52	53	54	55	56	57	58	59	60	61	62	63	64	65	66	67	68	69	70	71
1	24	✗	26	27	28	29	30	31	32	33	34	35	36	37	38	39	40	41	42	43	44	45	46	47
0	✗	1	2	3	4	5	6	7	8	9	10	11	12	13	14	15	16	17	18	19	20	21	22	23

UNPREDICTABLE FROG

>>> In the game, the frog starts from a different cell each time you click the green flag. You have seen how you can do this yourself by changing the cell and row number. How can we get our code to do this for us? We need the code to pick a random starting place each time. >>>

Open dragons5.sb2 in Scratch. Now when the green flag is clicked, we set the 'row' variable to pick at random any number between 0 and 17 (the row numbers on our grid), then the 'col' variable to pick any number between 0 and 23 (the column numbers on our grid). In this way we place the frog in any one of the 432 cells of the grid, completely at random.

AHA!

Not really random numbers ...

As computers only deal with true and false values they can't create a truly random number. They have to create a maths sum that appears random, instead. The sum needs to be complicated, or we might be able to predict what number it will pick. Can you guess what sum we did to create these numbers? Can you predict the next number?

1, 3, 5, 7, 9

Try to think up a sum that might be harder to predict.

>>> Being able to choose random numbers is very important in game design. In fact, most games couldn't work at all unless this was possible. >>>

Coding unplugged

People really can be random. Play this number guessing game with a friend. Think of a random number between 1 and 10. Ask your friend to guess the number. Tell them if their guess was less than or greater than your number. Your friend will be working like a computer's brain does, using comparison operators to decide which number to choose next depending on your answer. See how many guesses it takes for them to get it right. Now try choosing a number between 1 and 50!

23

ADDING DRAGONS!

Open dragons6.sb2 in Scratch. Now we have a frog appearing at random places on the screen. Using a similar method, we have also created the holes to appear at random around the screen. Our game board is ready, and it's time to bring on the dragons!

Using sub-routines

When we want to repeat the same thing at different points in our code we use a **sub-routine**. To get a sub-routine to run, we 'call' it. That just means that we call it by name in our code, and our code then fetches it and runs it.

1 You will see that we now have a sub-routine called 'CreateDragons'. We can enter how many dragons we want to create. We check that each dragon is not where the frog is. We also make sure that there is not a hole or another dragon in the same cell.

2 Once we have checked these things, we create a new dragon by making a clone of the dragon sprite. A clone is a copy.

Frog hunting

The dragons chase the frog. They do this by waiting for the frog to **broadcast** the message 'Chase'. Broadcasting messages is a way of one sprite talking to another. This message tells the dragons the frog's position The dragons then move towards that position by one square.

AHA!

Using costumes

You may not have noticed, but the dragons always face towards the frog. We do this by having four **costumes** (character poses), two facing to the left and two facing to the right. Click on the dragon sprite and then click on 'Costumes'. You will see the four different dragon poses that we use.

Think about it

To make a game work really well it may need a lot of code! When you are creating your own game, the code will make sense to you. You will be adding it, little by little, as you go. Someone else's code, like you are looking at now, can look pretty complicated! Just focus on the bits we are talking about and think about how you could use them in your game.

DID THE FROG DIE?

>>> Now that we have some holes and dragons, we need to think about what happens when the frog falls down a hole or runs into a dragon. Open dragons7.sb2 in Scratch. If you run the game, you will see that the frog dies if he walks into a hole or bumps into a dragon. >>>

Ending the game

If the frog dies, we need a way of stopping the game. We do this by creating a new variable called 'GameOn'. Look for it near the top of the right-hand long piece of code.

1 You will see that we initially set this variable to 1, when the green flag is clicked. We then add an IF statement to the main loop. This means that we will only move the frog IF the variable 'GameOn' is set to 1.

2 To check whether the frog has died, we use two more IF statements, run after any movement by the frog, like this:

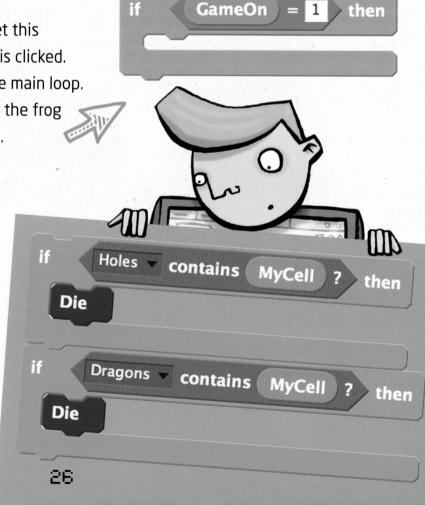

Sorry, you have died!

If the frog moves to a cell which already contains a hole or a dragon, it dies.

The game runs a sub-routine called 'Die', which looks like this:

This routine sets 'GameOn' to 0, meaning that the frog no longer moves; it also switches the backdrop to the 'die' screen and hides the frog. It then broadcasts a message named 'Delete'.

Message received

Messages are another way of one sprite talking to another. If you look in the code for the hole and dragon you will see that they look for this 'Delete' message. When it is received, the clones are deleted.

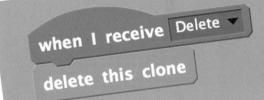

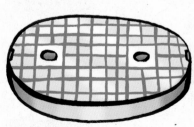

THE FINISHING TOUCHES

Now it's time to put the final tweaks to our Dragons game. What if, when you play the game, you get surrounded by dragons? It would be nice to have a way out, wouldn't it? Open dragons.sb2.

Escape!

Let's teleport! The teleport code looks like this:

When the T key is pressed, a new random cell is generated and the frog is sent there. For fun, we have made the frog glide to the spot while a sound plays! Then the game continues just like after any normal move.

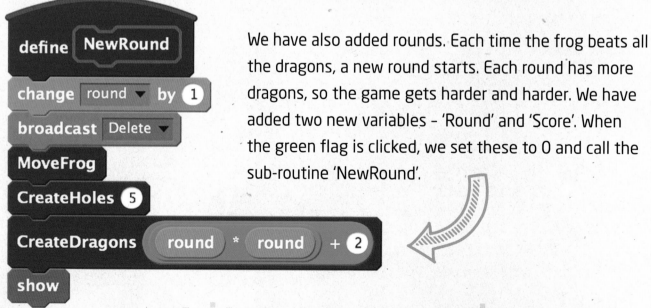

We have also added rounds. Each time the frog beats all the dragons, a new round starts. Each round has more dragons, so the game gets harder and harder. We have added two new variables – 'Round' and 'Score'. When the green flag is clicked, we set these to 0 and call the sub-routine 'NewRound'.

Testing, testing

When you create a game it is a good idea to get lots of people to test it for you. Code can get complicated, and you can get **bugs**. Bugs are when your code doesn't do exactly what you expect. If something isn't right, **debug** it. Check your code carefully to see what went wrong. Be careful that your changes do not cause another bug! Even the best programmers get bugs in their code, so don't worry if you do. Just test and fix as you go.

Try it!

Start creating your own game. It is best to try something simple first. One way is to look at some already-written code and make little changes. How about changing the sprites in the Dragons game? Choose your new hero from the 'New Sprite' menu. To give it the frog's code, right click your new sprite and click 'save to local file'. Save it somewhere easy to find.

Now click on the frog sprite, and then 'Costumes'. Click on the open folder symbol (left), point to the new sprite and import it. Delete the frog costume and you have a new hero! Now click the blue 'i' in the top left corner and type the name of your new hero.

Now use the skills you have learned to make your own great games. Have fun!

GLOSSARY

broadcast When one section of code sends a message to another part.

bug A mistake in a computer program.

code A set of instructions for a computer.

competitive Having a strong desire to win or be the best at something.

costumes In Scratch, these are the different positions each sprite is drawn in.

data Information for use in a computer.

debug To remove mistakes from a computer program.

grid A network of horizontal and vertical lines, often used for locating places

horizontal Running from side to side, parallel with the horizon; the top and bottom edges of this book are horizontal, for example.

operator A symbol that represents (stands for) an action, for example 'x' represents multiplication.

pixel Any one of the very small dots that together form the picture on a screen or computer monitor.

programmer Someone who writes the code for a computer program.

random Showing no clear pattern.

repeat until loop A series of instructions that are repeated until something you are waiting for happens.

sprite A simple, two-dimensional character that can be moved around within a larger scene.

sub-routine A set of instructions designed to perform a frequently used operation within a program.

variable A value that can change, depending on conditions or on information passed to the program.

vertical Running from top to bottom; a column in a table or a grid is vertical.

MORE INFORMATION

BOOKS

Vordeman, Carol. *Coding In Scratch For Games Made Easy (DK)* DK Children, London, UK: 2016.

Wainewright, Max. *Generation Code: I'm an Advanced Scratch Coder* Wayland, London, UK: 2017

WEBSITES

MIT's Scratch website, where you can download the program for free
https://scratch.mit.edu/about/

The Hour of Code website, which has tutorials that teach coding from beginner's level upwards
https://code.org/learn

VISIT

The **National Videogame Arcade**, Nottingham, houses thousands of video games, runs clubs and encourages hands-on experience of game-making.

The **Retro Computer Museum**, Leicester, is full of old gaming consoles. It holds gaming and computing events with access to retro computer equipment, and hosts educational visits and tours.

INDEX

ANSWERS

page 7   A scoreboard makes a game more competitive. Players will want to achieve as high a score as possible.

page 19 The statement uses AND logic: a move is only possible if the 7 key is pressed AND there is enough space.

page 21 The number '0' is also counted in both cases.

AHA!